Palestine Dances!

Palestine Dances!

FOLK DANCES OF PALESTINE

AS SET DOWN BY

CORINNE CHOCHEM AND

MURIEL ROTH

DRAWINGS BY MOSES SOYER · PHOTOGRAPHS BY JOHN MILLS, JR.

Behrman's Jewish Book House
PUBLISHERS, NEW YORK
1941

Foreword

℄ AGAINST THE SETTING SUN, in the fields near a kevutzah[1] in Palestine, a group of young halutzim[2] are dancing. All day long they have worked hard on the land. The morrow brings another day of toil. Still, their zest for life is undaunted and their spirit undimmed.

The dancers move joyously round in a circle—strong, sure and impassioned. Their voices are raised in vibrant song. Their rhythm quickens. Their tempo becomes more staccato. Now the circle breaks and another halutz joins in. The circle closes and the dance goes round, faster and faster.

Another group of workers returns from the fields, tired and begrimed. Suddenly they see the dancers. They hail them with a shout, throw down their tools, dash to the pump, wash their faces and fling themselves into the now swift moving circle. This is the Horah—the dance of new Palestine, happy, young and full of hope!

This is the Horah! Where did it come from? It is known that all dances have their origin in primitive ritual. Many of the earlier ones were agricultural dances in which people would join together to celebrate the harvest. They would use patterns such as leaps, high jumps and the upward movement of the arms to symbolize the growth of the grain. It was believed that the higher the leap, the higher the grain would grow. It is these simple agricultural dances which were preserved, with variations, through the centuries and served as the matrix for many of the European folk dances.

Horah is a Croatian-Serbian word meaning "tempo" or "movement." It is also the name of a middle nineteenth-century Balkan folk-dance, the main patterns of which are, similarly, leaps and high jumps, to suggest and induce the high growth of the corn.

The Sephardic Jews, who, as exiles from Spain after the Inquisition, had migrated to the Balkans and settled there, absorbed this dance into their own ceremony. It became for them a dance of joy, to celebrate their *simhas*[3]—their weddings and their holidays.

The Horah now took on a more enclosed—an indoor—character and consequently became more restrained, since it was being danced within their homes and synagogues by an urban people, dressed, for the most part, in tight fitting clothes and shoes. In time, many of the Sephardim journeyed to Palestine, bringing this dance along with them.

Meanwhile, the Ashkenazic Jews, in Roumania, Poland, Russia and other East European countries, were dancing the Bulgar, a popular Jewish wedding dance. The Bulgar is a development of the same agricultural dance as the Horah. It too underwent a restraining influence in the crowded ghetto milieu, but its quality probably became more expressively emotional, due to the strong impact and fervor of the Hassidim.

In the early part of the twentieth century, the halutzim who came to Palestine from Eastern Europe revived the old Sephardic Horah and combined it with their own dance traditions. Furthermore, as the Horah is danced today in Palestine, it seems to have an even more authentic color, since it has now reverted to vocal instead of instrumental accompaniment, and is once again danced under the open sky, bringing it still closer to its original agricultural source.

Like many early folk dances, the Palestinian Horah is circular in form. It begins slowly but vigorously at an even, measured tempo. Its movements are strong and deliberate, and, in the manner of most primitive and oriental dances, it builds on a fast exhilarated crescendo to a continuing, excited whirl.

Moreover, though never losing its force and dynamic rhythms, the Horah subtly fuses the healthy energy of the youthful builders with the mystic ecstasy and abandon of their

Hassidic forbears, the exaggerated, sensuous movements giving to the dance new, rich and colorful overtones.

But what matters the story of this dance! The important thing is that after long hours of hard labor in the fields and factories, a people engaged in the upbuilding of a new land find new enthusiasm, new strength and new hope with which to face the difficult years ahead when they dance the Horah, their dance of affirmation.

❡ IT IS NECESSARY to note that while this book describes but two versions of the Horah, many of the other dances derive extensively from it, and, at the same time, suggest various folk dances of other countries, among which are the English, Swedish, Russian, Polish and Arabic, where Jews have lived for long periods.

❡ WITH DEEP DEVOTION, I dedicate this book to the Histadruth Hanoar Haivri. I also wish to express my heartfelt gratitude to my collaborator, Muriel Roth, whose extensive musical knowledge, untiring cooperation, and sympathetic understanding made this book possible.

I am particularly indebted to Moshe Davis and Leah Klepper for their constant assistance and encouragement; to Chaim Kieval for his aid in the translation and transliteration of the Hebrew verses; and, above all, to the following members of the Rikkud Ami Dance Group of the Histadruth Hanoar Haivri, who posed for the photographs and the drawings: Sylvia Fiacre, Goldie Fogel, Hilda Gelbard and Ruth Shul.

CORINNE CHOCHEM

❦ AUTHOR'S NOTE: These dances, like most folk dances, continue by repetition as long as the group or the leader wishes. The Scher is the only one which progresses through a long pattern of steps leading to a climax and an end.

Where it seems necessary, the step patterns and the music are correlated with numbers, such as (1) (2). In general the steps fit so easily and so naturally with the music that the correlation is only indicated by the section, such as 'First eight measures.'

There are always different versions of folk dances and folk tunes, no one of which is necessarily the best or most correct. We have tried in this book to set down accurately the most common version and have not complicated the usefulness of the book with allusions to other versions.

The English lyrics give the substance and the spirit of the Hebrew but are in no sense literal translations. Their meter does not conform to that of the music. Do not try to sing the English!

C. C. and M. R.

[1] A cooperative colony in Palestine   [2] Pioneers   [3] Joyous occasions

TO SEE PALESTINE DANCE IS TO SEE A PEOPLE REBORN!

Table of Contents

Palestine Dances!

Y'minah, y'minah

The Music

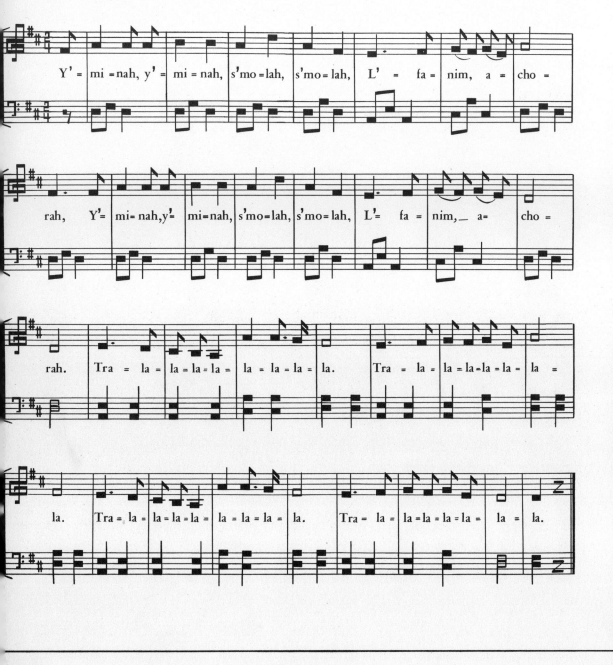

יְמִינָה, יְמִינָה, שְׂמֹאלָה, שְׂמֹאלָה,   Right, right, left, left,
לְפָנִים, אֲחוֹרָה,   Forward, backward.
יְמִינָה, יְמִינָה, שְׂמֹאלָה, שְׂמֹאלָה,   Right, right, left, left,
לְפָנִים, אֲחוֹרָה,   Forward, backward.
טְרַ, לַלַלַלַלַלַל.   Tra, la, la, la, la.

The Dance

℘ FORMATION: This dance is performed entirely in couples. At the start, couples form one large circle, all dancers facing the center. Each couple joins right and left hands, crossed in back.

℘ THE STEPS: First eight bars: Take three steps to the right: right, left, right, (the left foot stepping behind the right). Kick the left foot across in front of the right while hopping on the right. Then three steps to the left: left, right, left, (the right foot stepping behind the left). Kick the right foot across in front of the left while hopping on the left. Now the couples move forward toward the center of the circle, starting with the right foot: step—hop—step—hop. Then they move backward to place; again starting with right foot: step—hop—step—hop.

Second eight bars: Repeat the steps of the first eight bars.

Third eight bars: Couples turn to the right and follow each other in the circle, stepping forward with right foot: step—hop—step—hop to the end of the music. These sixteen step-hops are done in a slightly slower tempo to allow for greater emphasis.

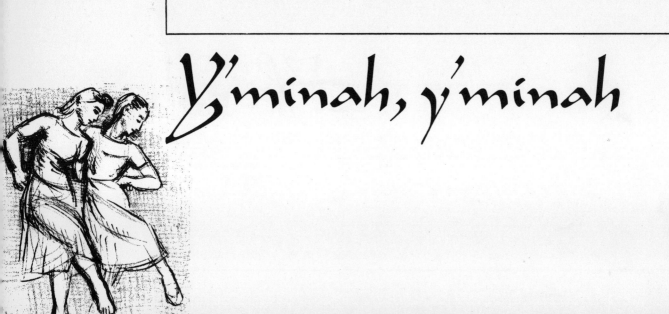

Y'minah, y'minah

The Dance

❧ FORMATION: Dancers form a circle with hands on nearest shoulders of the dancers on either side.

❧ THE STEPS: First three bars: Take three steps to the right: right, left, right, (the left foot is placed behind the right). Then kick the left foot in front of the right while hopping on the right. Take one step left with the left foot and kick the right foot across in front of the left while hopping on the left. Notice that the pattern is in six counts: step, step, step, kick, step, kick. Continue this same pattern throughout the dance.

Begin the Horah slowly in order to establish the rhythm, and keep the tempo slow until everyone feels the rhythm together. Then accelerate gradually. Although the dance becomes very exciting, the dancers should never lose control nor allow the circle to break. Anyone exhausted may leave the circle, but the other dancers must close the circle immediately.

If the group is very large, divide the dancers into two circles, one outside circle and one smaller inside circle. The two circles may move in the same or in opposite directions.

There are many different Horah melodies, although only four, to be found in the pages immediately following, have been included in this book. The dance itself, as described above, is alike for all these four, as for all Horah melodies.

Horah

Horah · SOV'VUNI

The Music

So=v'=vu=ni, la=hat esh bo=er=et Ra=k'=du=li shir ya=chid,—

Zeh ha=ze=mer, zeh v'=ain a=cher od, V'ain a=cher od l'=ta=mid.

fine

Tov, tov, tov, tov, tov, tov, Tov ha=ze=mer ad ain sof.

Lo yit=tam,— lo yach=lof Bil'=va=ve=nu

ha=ko=dei=ach Mit=tla=mim u=miy=ya=rei=ach.

d. c. al fine

סוֹבְבוּנִי, לַהַט אֵשׁ בּוֹעֶרֶת.	*I want fire all around me!*
רַקְדוּ לִי שִׁיר יָחִיד,	*Here's the melody to dance to—*
זֶה הַזֶּמֶר, זֶה וְאֵין אַחֵר עוֹד,	*It's the only song there is.*
וְאֵין אַחֵר עוֹד לְתָמִיד.	*Sing it always!*
טוֹב, טוֹב, טוֹב, טוֹב, טוֹב, טוֹב,	*Good! A good song*
טוֹב הַזֶּמֶר עַד אֵין סוֹף.	*Is a song without an end.*
לֹא יִתַּם, לֹא יַחֲלוֹף	*We'll never forget it.*
בִּלְבָבֵנוּ הַקּוֹדֵחַ	*We'll never forget it.*
מִתְּלָמִים וּמְיָרֵחַ.	

Horah · SHURU HABITU

The Music

Shu=ru ha=bi=tu, u=r'=u Mah ga=dol ha=yom ha= zeh,

Esh yo=ke=det be=cha=zeh, V'=ha=mach=r'ei=shah Shuv po=la=chat ba=sa= deh.

Shuv po=la=chat ba=sa= deh. Et, ma=kosh, tu=riy=yah v'=kil=shon,

Hit=lak=du bi=s'=a=rah V'=nad=li=kah shuv, Shuv et ha=a=da=mah,

B'=shal=he=vet y'=ro= kah. B'=shal=he=vet y'=ro= kah.

שׁוּרוּ, הַבִּיטוּ וּרְאוּ — Look! The plow breaks the soil.

מַה גָּדוֹל הַיּוֹם הַזֶּה, — See

אֵשׁ יוֹקֶדֶת בְּחָזֶה, — The beauty of the day.

וְהַמַּחֲרֵשָׁה — Breath quickens—

שׁוּב פּוֹלַחַת בַּשָּׂדֶה. — The spade, the fork, the rake, the hoe

אֵת, מַכּוֹשׁ, טוּרִיָּה וְקִלְשׁוֹן, — In happy unison, skillfully

הִתְלַכְּדוּ בִּסְעָרָה — Quicken the earth.

וְנַדְלִיקָה שׁוּב,

שׁוּב אֶת הָאֲדָמָה,

בְּשַׁלְהֶבֶת יְרוֹקָה.

Horah · CHANITAH

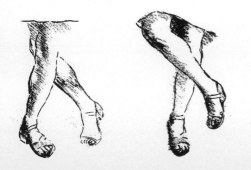

The Music

Lai=lah mis=ta=rei'=a, eish min he=ha=rim Ei mi=sham bo=kei'=a Ze=mer gib=bo=rim.

Eish li=bi hil=hi=tah, Eish li=bi tal=hiv, Lach a=ni,Cha=ni=tah, Lach sa=viv, sa=viv.

Ho=ra=tei=nu, E=res g'vu=ra=tei=nu, Ho=ra=tei=nu, E=res g'vu=ra tei=nu,

Go=n'=ni, go=n'=ni a=lei=nu. Go=n'=ni, go=n'=ni a=lei=nu, a=lei=nu.

ritard.

לַיְלָה מִשְׂתָּרֵעַ, Night fills all the valleys

אֵשׁ מִן הֶהָרִים, And fires are lit on the hills.

אֵי־מִשָּׁם בּוֹקֵעַ Heroes are singing far away.

זֶמֶר גִּבּוֹרִים. I feel as though my heart were kindled—

אֵשׁ לִבִּי הִלְהִיטָה, My heart bursts aflame.

אֵשׁ לִבִּי תַּלְהִיב, Chanitah, my village, I love you!

לָךְ אֲנִי, חֲנִיתָה, Chanitah!

לָךְ סָבִיב, סָבִיב. Come, friends, and let us dance!

הוֹרָתֵנוּ,

עֶרֶשׂ גְּבוּרָתֵנוּ,

גּוֹנְנִי עָלֵינוּ.

Horah • ALI, ALI

The Music

Ba = nu bli kol va = chol,
Tzei = na la ma' = a = gal,

A = nu a = ni = yei et = mol,
Ten = na shir miz = mor la = dal,

La = nu ha = go = ral ma = sar
Hen = nah ne = es = fu lir = kod

Et mil = yo = nei ha = ma = char.
B'nei ha = o = ni v' = ha shod.

Ho = rah, a = li, a = li!

Esh had = li = ki b' = lei = li,

T'ho = rah ra = bat o = rah,

ho = rah m' = du = rah!

צֵא נָא לַמַּעְגָּל,

תֵּן נָא שִׁיר מִזְמוֹר לַדָּל;

הֵנָּה נֶאֶסְפוּ לִרְקֹד

בְּנֵי הָעֹנִי וְהַשֹּׁד!

בָּאנוּ בְּלִי כֹל וָכֹל,

אָנוּ עֲנִיֵּי־אֶתְמוֹל,

לָנוּ הַגּוֹרָל מָסַר

אֶת מִלְיוֹנֵי הַמָּחָר.

הוֹרָה, עֲלִי, עֲלִי! אֵשׁ הַדְלִיקִי בְּלֵילִי,

טְהוֹרָה רַבַּת אוֹרָה, הוֹרָה מְדוּרָה!

We were poor—we came empty handed.

But that's over now.

We'll come out ahead—a people of millions.

Let's dance the Horah! Let's leap!

Light the fires in the night.

Light the bright fires.

Let's dance!

The Dance

❧ FORMATION: Dancers stand in a circle with hands on nearest shoulders of the dancers on either side—the usual Horah formation.

❧ THE STEPS: First eight bars: Facing a little toward the right, take two steps toward the right: right, left, and jump with feet together. Then facing a little toward the left, take two steps toward the left: left, right, and jump with feet together. Repeat right and left.

Second eight bars: Take twelve steps (two to a bar) to the right with alternating feet, stepping out with the right foot, placing the left foot behind the right on half-toe. On the seventh bar, continue to move right with one step on the right foot. Kick the left foot across in front of the right while hopping on the right. Then step left with the left foot and kick the right across the left while hopping on the left.

Third eight bars: Repeat the second eight bars with exactly the same pattern but move to the left. Since the right foot is free at the end of the preceding eight bars, start the pattern by swinging the right foot to half-toe behind the left.

As in the case of other Horahs, establish the rhythm by beginning slowly, and then gradually accelerate the tempo.

Horah variation • HINNEH MAH T

The Music

הִנֵּה מַה־טּוֹב וּמַה־נָּעִים
שֶׁבֶת אַחִים גַּם יָחַד!

What a good thing it is
For people to dwell happily together!

Achshav

The Music

עַכְשָׁו, עַכְשָׁו, בְּעֵמֶק יִזְרְעָאל.

עַכְשָׁו, עַכְשָׁו, בְּעֵמֶק יִזְרְעָאל.

טוּמְבָּה, טוּמְבָּה, טוּמְבָּה בְּעֵמֶק יִזְרְעָאל.

טוּמְבָּה, טוּמְבָּה, טוּמְבָּה בְּעֵמֶק יִזְרְעָאל.

Home, at last, in Emek Yizr'el.

Tumbah, tumbah, tumbah, in Emek Yizr'el.

Achshav

The Dance

℀ FORMATION: Dancers stand side by side in couples forming one line. Each couple joins right and left hands, crossed in back.

℀ THE STEPS: First eight bars: Jump to the right on the right foot (1) and immediately take two steps in place: left, right. Repeat to left (2), beginning with left foot. Dropping hands, each dancer then makes a complete turn separately in place in three steps, turning away from partner. At (3), join hands again crossed in back and repeat the steps beginning again with a jump to the right and finishing with the turn in place.

Next four bars: Face partner and take hands. Couples take three slides, all moving in the same direction. At (4) raise hands high without losing hold of partner's hands and make a complete turn in place in four steps—each dancer turning separately and turning under own and partner's hands.

Next four bars: Quickly place right hand on partner's waist with left hand held high, as in the photographs. In this position, each couple turns in place in seven running steps. The couples then return to the original position, standing in one line with right and left hands joined and crossed in back, in order to repeat the dance.

Tscherkessia

The Music

Tra = la = la = la = la = la = la = la = la = la = la = la = la = la = la = la = la = la = la = la = la.

Tra = la = la = la = la = la = la = la = la = la = la = la = la = la = la = la = la = la = la = la = la.

Tscherkessia

The Dance

℄ FORMATION: Dancers stand in two equal lines facing each other, hands around one another's waists.

℄ THE STEPS: First eight bars: Keeping the left foot in place, step forward with the right foot (1) and then backward with the right foot (2). Repeat four times. As each step is taken with the right foot, the left knee tends to bend to give flexibility. Note the exaggerated movements in the photographs. While stepping forward, the body leans very much forward; while stepping backward, the body leans back as far as possible.

Second eight bars: The two lines each move to the right with sixteen steps, the right foot stepping directly to the right, the left foot stepping to the right behind the right foot. The two lines, instead of moving away from each other while traveling with this step, continue to face each other because they travel in a circular pattern.

This dance should be started in a slow but very steady tempo. Each repetition is a little faster until a climax of great excitement is reached.

After the dance is well under way, variations are sometimes used for the second eight bars. The dancer on the extreme right of either line acts as leader in introducing variations. The following are four suggestions, by no means an exhaustive list.

1. Sixteen scissor kicks in front.

2. Sixteen scissor kicks in back.

3. A combination of scissor kicks in front and back.

4. Eight slow skips to the right (one to a bar).

The Dance

❡ FORMATION: Dancers stand in two equal lines facing each other, with hands on nearest shoulders of the dancers on either side. The dancer on the right end of each line acts as leader and usually holds a handkerchief high with his right hand. The waving of the handkerchief seems to emphasize the accents of the music and the excitement of the dance.

❡ THE STEPS: The complete pattern of steps for this dance is only four bars long. It is in eight movements, each on a beat, two to a bar.

1. Extend left foot forward, with heel on the floor.

2. Return left foot to place beside the right foot.

3. Extend right foot forward, with heel raised just off the floor.

4. Raise right foot in the air with bent knee while hopping on the left foot.

5. Take one step to right with the right foot.

6. Take one step to the right with the left foot crossing over in front of the right.

7. Jump with feet together, body turned slightly toward left and knees bent.

8. Jump with feet together, body turned slightly toward right and knees bent.

The dance continues by repetition of this pattern of steps. The two lines of dancers, instead of moving away from each other while each travels to the right, continue to face each other because they travel in a circular pattern. Compare with the movement of the two lines in the *Tscherkessia*.

This dance starts slowly—the movements, especially the two jumps, are done somewhat loosely. The tempo increases gradually as the accents become more marked and the movements more emphatic and exaggerated, and the dance is finally a whirlwind of excitement.

Debka

The Music

Z'chartihah

The Music

זְכַרְתִּיהָ, יְמִימָה,
בַּת צִיּוֹן הִיא תְּמִימָה.

I remember Yemimah,
Zion's daughter,
Perfect one.

Z'chartihah

The Dance

❡ FORMATION: This dance is performed throughout by separate couples, facing in one direction in a circle, or standing in a line. Each couple joins outside hands in front and puts inside hands around partner's waist. (Almost a social dancing position, as in the first photograph illustrating this dance).

❡ THE STEPS: First eight bars: Point outside foot forward (1); then place the same foot crossed over inside foot (2). Walk three steps forward, (3) (4) (5): outside foot, inside foot, outside foot. On the last step, each person turns separately to face the opposite direction while changing the position of the hands accordingly. Repeat from the beginning in this direction and again reverse the direction with the last step. Each couple will now be in its original place and facing the original direction.

Second eight bars: Repeat steps for the first eight bars.

First eight bars of music repeated: Each couple joins right hands, facing each other as in a handshake. Jump toward partner and away from partner. Repeat three times, one jump to a bar. Then dropping hands, make a circle around partner in four running steps—passing partner on right first, then back to back, and finishing in place.

Second eight bars of music repeated: Repeat the six jumps toward and away from partner, this time holding left hands. Again drop hands and make a circle around partner, this time passing partner on left first, then back to back and finishing in place.

Note that a repetition of the music is necessary to complete the steps of this dance once.

The Dance

℃ FORMATION: Dancers join hands in a circle, except one man in the center.

℃ THE STEPS: First eight bars: Those in the circle, holding hands, take sixteen slow steps (two to a bar) to the right. The man in the center walks in the opposite direction and finishes in front of a dancer whom he leads into the center as his chosen partner.

Those in the circle now stop walking and clap (twice to a bar) during the rest of the dance.

Second eight bars: The man and his partner take four step-hops to the right, in a circle in place with the right hand of each dancer on partner's right shoulder, then four step-hops to the left, again in circle in place with the left hand of each dancer on partner's left shoulder. Repeat right and left. The couple claps once as it starts each group of four step-hops.

The man then returns to a place in the circle, and the dancer previously chosen as his partner starts the dance again.

This dance is done in a very gay manner. The steps are simple and easily learned and should be done very rhythmically and with a great deal of spirit.

The simplicity of the steps makes the dance an excellent beginning for an evening of folk dancing, and the melody can be sung with "tra-la-la" instead of the words while dancing.

Niggun

The Music

יְרוּשָׁלַיִם עִיר הַקֹּדֶשׁ,

שָׁם תֵּשֵׁב בְּלִי אֹכֶל כָּל הַחֹדֶשׁ,

תְּבַקֵּשׁ עֲבוֹדָה,

אֲבָל לֹא תִמְצָא לְךָ מְאוּמָה.

הָה, הָה, כָּזֹאת הֲרֵי הִיא אַרְצֵנוּ,

זֹאת הָאָרֶץ, אֶרֶץ אֲבוֹתֵינוּ.

בָּה חָפְשִׁים כָּל אַחֵינוּ,

אֵין גָּלוּת, יֵשׁ רַק חֵרוּת.

Jerusalem, the holy city!

One needn't worry about eating,

One needn't worry about work.

That's how it's now in our country,

The land of our fathers.

We're all free now.

It's freedom, not exile.

Ura amchah

The Music

עוּרָה, עַמְּךָ, עוּרָה, הַקִּבּוּץ.
חַג־פּוּרִים נָחוּץ.
חַג־פּוּרִים הוּא יוֹם־הַדִּין
בְּחַיֵּי הַקִּבּוּץ.

Wake up, you people! Wake up, you settlers!
Let's celebrate this Purim Day.
This is the day that we triumphed.
Purim means that to our colony.

The Dance

℃ FORMATION: Dancers form in couples, partners standing side by side, but facing in opposite directions. Each couple joins hands, crisscrossed in back, as in the drawing.

℃ THE STEPS: First ten bars: Each couple turns right in place with twenty running steps. At the seventh bar, the dancers, as they continue to turn, hook together their inside arms and raise their outside hands high.

Next eight bars: Face partner and hold hands. As in bleking (*), hop on right foot and at the same time extend the left. Then hop on left and extend the right. Repeat, hopping on the right and then the left foot. (This is done fast—twice to a bar). At (1), partners separate with four slides to the right. At (2), each does four bleking steps beginning with right foot extended. Then four slides to the left, returning to position, facing partner.

Last eight bars: Joining hands, take four bleking steps beginning with left foot extended. Then with hands still joined, turn right in a complete circle in place with partner in four running steps. Repeat, with four bleking steps beginning with the right foot extended and then turn to the left on the four running steps.

(*) When partners do the bleking step facing each other and holding hands, they use their hands in a backwards and forwards motion which corresponds to that of the feet. (See photograph).

Ura amchah

The Dance

❆ FORMATION: Dancers stand side by side in couples, forming one single line. However, the boys face in one direction and the girls in the opposite. Arms are crisscrossed by all in back, and the hands clasped, as in the photograph.

❆ THE STEPS: First eight bars: Each couple turns right in place with sixteen running steps and finishes in its original position. Partners drop hands and face each other to continue the dance—so that a line of boys faces a line of girls.

Second eight bars: (Same music much slower). Everyone takes three slides to the right and kicks the left foot in front of right while hopping on the right. (The lines move in opposite directions on the floor.) Then take three slides to the left and kick the right foot across the left. Repeat this step—to the right and to the left and finish facing partner.

Third eight bars: Each couple turns in place with four step-hops, beginning with the right foot. On the first beat (1), each dancer claps his hands once and then places his right hand, raised high, palm to palm against his partner's while continuing the step-hops. Then take four step-hops, turning in the other direction, again beginning with a clap (2) and continuing with left hands raised high and placed palm to palm. At the end of this step, the couples must quickly return to their original position in order to be ready to start the dance again.

Ari-ara

Ari-ara

The Music

The Dance

❦ FORMATION: Dancers stand in a circle in the Horah formation—with hands on nearest shoulders of the dancers on either side.

❦ THE STEPS: First four bars: Take three steps to the right—right, left, right—the left foot stepping behind the right. Kick the left foot in front of right while hopping on the right (the first part of the Horah step). Then take three jumps: first with the right foot crossed in front of the left, then with feet apart, then with feet together. (See drawings.) This step continues throughout the dance.

Begin this dance slowly so that a feeling of group rhythm is established. Then gradually accelerate the tempo until an exciting climax is reached.

Pa'am achat variation

The Music

Pa'am a=chat ba= | chur ya=tza | el ha= | k'vish. | Pa'am a=chat ba= | chur ya=tza, U=
Shim'ee= na cha= | vee=va= tee, | hu a= | mar, | Shim'ee = na cha= | vee=va=tee,____

va=chu=rah hu | sham ma=tza, Al | yad ha=ma=cha= | neh, | Ha= | yah zeh ba=sa= | deh.
Mah=do =fe=ket | lib=ba =tee! Al | yad ha=ma=cha= | neh, | Ha= | yah zeh ba=sa= | deh.

פַּעַם אַחַת בָּחוּר יָצָא אֶל הַכְּבִישׁ.	A fellow went down the road once,
פַּעַם אַחַת בָּחוּר יָצָא	A fellow went down the road,
וּבַחוּרָה הוּא שָׁם מָצָא.	And there he found a pretty girl—
עַל יַד הַמַּחֲנֶה,	Near the village, in the fields.
הָיָה זֶה בַּשָּׂדֶה.	"Listen to me, my love," he said
שִׁמְעִי נָא, חֲבִיבָתִי, הוּא אָמַר,	"Listen to me, my love.
שִׁמְעִי נָא, חֲבִיבָתִי,	Hear how fast my heart is beating."
מַה דוֹפֶקֶת לִבָּתִי!	It was near the village, in the fields.
עַל יַד הַמַּחֲנֶה,	
הָיָה זֶה בַּשָּׂדֶה.	

Scher

The Music

Scher

The Dance

❈ FORMATION: This dance is performed by four couples standing in a square, one couple on each side of the square, the boy on the girl's right.

❈ THE STEPS: First eight bars: Everyone joins hands and takes eight running steps to the right, then eight running steps to the left, finishing in place. (This step seems to make a circle. Be sure to get back into a square again, with one couple on each side of the square.) Second eight bars: Two of the couples, facing each other, cross to each other's place on four running steps. One of these couples raises clasped hands high (forming an arch as in the photograph) to allow the other couple to go through as they cross. Then the other two couples do the same, changing places on four running steps. Then the pattern is repeated: the first two couples cross again and return to their original places and the second two couples do the same. Throughout, the standing couples clap hands in accompaniment.

From this point on, the music continues by repetition, and the steps do not fit in any fixed way to the music. The steps are done sometimes to one part, sometimes to another part of the music. Consequently the dance steps are given without any indication of the corresponding bars of the music.

Moving on vigorous step-hops, one boy makes a complete circle in place with his partner. This turning is done with the right hand of each dancer on partner's right shoulder. Then the boy, continuing the step-hops, joins the girl in the next couple and makes a circle in place with her. This turning is done with the left hand of each dancer on partner's left shoulder. The boy, still moving on the step-hops, returns to his own partner and turns her, again with right hands on right shoulders. The boy then goes on to the girl in the opposite couple, turns her with left hands on left shoulders; returns to his own partner, turns her with right hands on right shoulders; and then turns the girl in the remaining couple with left hands on left shoulders. Note that the boy continues to move all the time with step-hops while each girl only moves while the boy is turning her. Note also that the boy alternates hands with the turnings since he always turns his own partner with right hands on right shoulders and the girls in the other couples with left hands on left shoulders.

Dance continued on page 55

Scher

As at the beginning of the dance, join hands and take eight running steps to the right and eight to the left. This step always seems to make a circle. Be sure to return to a square formation again, with one couple on each side of the square.

The girl who is the partner of the boy who has already done the turning now follows the same pattern: she turns her partner, then the boy in the next couple, then her partner, the boy in the opposite couple, her partner, and the boy in the remaining couple. As before, she turns her partner with right hands on right shoulders and the other boys with left hands on left shoulders.

Repeat the steps for the first eight bars of the dance: i.e., the running in a circle.

The boy in the next couple goes through the same steps, turning his partner and the other girls.

Repeat the steps for the first eight bars of the dance: i.e., the running in a circle.

The girl in this couple goes through the same steps, turning her partner and the other boys.

Repeat the running in a circle.

Continue with the boy and the girl of the third and fourth couples doing the turning. Remember that the step used for the first eight bars of the dance is done between the turning pattern of each dancer, and be sure to reform a square after each repetition of this running in a circle.

When the last girl has finished turning the boys, couples form a square with partners facing each other. Thus the boys face left and the girls right. Each dancer clasps right hands with his partner and, moving forward on step-hops, passes his partner on the left. Then he passes the next dancer he meets on the right—with left hands clasped. Thus each dancer continues to move forward while extending right and left hands alternately to each successive dancer whom he meets. (See photograph).

For a variation, this figure, which is called "the grand right and left," may be done with right hand on partner's right shoulder, left hand on partner's left shoulder, and so forth, instead of with hands clasped.

Kum bachur atzel

Kum bachur atzel

The Dance

℄ FORMATION: Dancers join hands in a circle, except one person who pretends to sleep on the ground in the center. Those in the circle attempt to arouse the lazy one in the center with their singing and dancing. The one in the center stretches, yawns and improvises movements to suggest waking up slowly.

℄ THE STEPS: First eight bars: Those in the circle hold hands and stamp in place: right, left, right, (1) (2) (3). Then take two slow slides to the right (4) (5). Then stamp in place: left, right, left, and take two slides to the left.

Second eight bars: Those in the circle lunge forward with the right foot and point to the person in the center (6). At (7), bring the foot back in place and put hands on hips. For the next two bars (8), make work movements(*) with the arms, while stamping in place: right, left, right. Repeat.

Third eight bars: Turn right (a half turn) to the outside with three stamps, (9), pretending to play a bugle. At (10), turn left (a half turn) in three stamps with hands on hips, thus facing center. Repeat the above, turning in the opposite directions, left to outside and right to facing center.

While those in the circle are doing these steps, the one in the center slowly wakes up as described above. At the end, he points to someone in the circle to take his place in the center, and the dance starts again.

This dance is especially enjoyed by young children.

(*) A suggested work movement: three large, vigorous circles with arms and clenched fists, done in front of the face on a plane parallel to the chest: left, right, left. If the leader wishes, he can encourage each child to make up his own work movement.

Pa'am achat

The Music

Pa'am a=chat ba=chur ya=tza El ha=mo=sha=vah, Pa'am a=chat ba=chur ya=tza, Ba=chu=rah hu sham ma=tza. Hey! Up=tza=za tra=la=la, Up=tza=za tra=la=la Bo=i hei=nah yal=dah V' nir=kod=na. Hey! na.

פַּעַם אַחַת בָּחוּר יָצָא אֶל הַמּוֹשָׁבָה,
פַּעַם אַחַת בָּחוּר יָצָא, בַּחוּרָה הוּא שָׁם מָצָא.
הֵי! אוּפְּ-צָ-צָ תְּרַ לַ לַ
בּוֹאִי הֵנָּה יַלְדָּה וְנִרְקֹד-נָא.

A fellow went out to the village once,
Out to the village he went.
And there he met a pretty girl.
Hey!
Uptza-za, tra-la-la,
Uptza-za, tra-la-la,
Come to me, my lassie
Come, and let us dance.

61

Pa'am achat

The Dance

❦ FORMATION: Dancers join hands in a big circle, except one boy who stands in the center. Those in the circle walk first right, then left while the boy in the center walks in the opposite direction, as he decides which girl in the circle to select as a partner. As he beckons to her, those in the circle stop walking and stand in place, accompanying the rest of the dance with clapping. The girl joins him in the center, beckoning to him in turn. Then they link arms and dance together gaily until he returns to a place in the circle leaving the girl to start the dance again.

❦ THE STEPS: First eight bars: Those in the circle walk eight steps to the right then eight steps to the left. The person in the center at the same time walks eight steps to the left, eight steps to the right. At the exclamation "Hey", he points to the chosen partner, and the circle stops in place.

Second eight bars: The boy, beckoning to the girl, takes four skips backward as the girl takes four skips toward him. Then they reverse the step: she beckons, skipping backward, and he skips toward her. At (1), the couple claps once, links right arms and takes four step-hops together, turning to the right in a circle in place: right foot, left foot, etc.

Third eight bars: Repeat the steps for the second eight bars, this time linking left arms and turning left. At the end, the boy must return to a place in the circle quickly so that the dance may begin again with the girl in the center of the circle.

This dance is as suitable for a group of adults as for children and can be used successfully with either a small or a large number. Although the directions are given for boys and girls, the dance does not require an equal number of each nor even a mixed group.

CORINNE CHOCHEM *was born in Russia and came to this country as a child. She studied under the foremost exponents of the dance in this country and in Europe, and combines a rich Hebrew background with the formal techniques of modern dancing. While visiting Palestine, she studied the folk dance forms of the halutzim. She has performed frequently both here and abroad, is a talented lecturer, and now leads a Jewish dance group of her own.*